FROM BROKE TO BANK: STEP BY STEP GUIDE TO HOME BASED DENTAL CLINIC CONSULTING BUSINESS

Soham M.

Copyright © 2018

All rights reserved. No part of this book may be reproduced or transmitted in any form or by any means, electronic or mechanical, including photocopying, recording or by any information storage and retrieval system without written permission of the publisher, except for the inclusion of brief quotations in a review.

Disclaimer:

Please read the Disclaimer carefully before you read this book. You accept and agree to be bound and abide by the Disclaimer. The information contained on this book is for educational and informational purposes only. The information contained on this book is not intended as, and shall not be understood or construed as, professional advice.

The brand names or logos discussed in this book are property of their respective owners.

Introduction 5
Why dentists need marketing consultants? 7
Your Job As A Marketing Consultant 9
Assessing Your Client 12
Prepare a Free Report 15
Planning for expansion 17
Approaching A Client..19
Marketing Strategies you can recommend to your clients 21
How To Generate Word of Mouth Buzz 26
Harnessing The Power Of Testimonials 28

Introduction

Dentists are trained to treat the problems of teeth; they are very good at it. The dental clinic just like any other business requires a steady stream of clients. The job of dentists is a specialist job, hence they have very little time to devote for marketing of their clinic or build a brand. The competition for dental clinics has increased with the advent of internet. Today there is even more need than ever for dental clinics to adopt a marketing strategy that can help them market the clinic effectively.

As a consultant you want the dental clinics to choose you. This book focuses on the issues faced by the dental clinics and how to implement the strategies that increase the business of dental clinics. You must be familiar with the concepts of marketing and utilizing the same to help your clients grow their business. You can offer your services to track the competition. You can check the websites of competing clinics, write down their offers, and study various products. This will help you to formulate effective marketing strategy for your client.

Why dentists need marketing consultants?

Marketing and branding are a significant part of the dental practice's success, stability and development. But the question is who should manage them? A dentist or a Professional Marketer?

A dentist certainly can't do it all himself. He could allocate the task to his manager or he may hire an in-house marketer. The better option is to outsource the entire process of marketing and brand communications to an external agency that specializes in delivering results.

Listed below are six reasons that make sense for a dental clinic to hire professional marketing consultants.

1. Savings of Cash

Dental clinics pays a fixed cost each month, and hire a marketing consultant that specializes in online as well as offline marketing. It makes handling cash-flow easier, and if for any reason the dental clinic feels to cutback or drop the campaign, they can do this quickly without the stress of additional expenses.

2. When a dental clinic hires a professional marketing consultant, they are assured of hiring established and reliable marketing expert. If they decide to delegate the work to their in-house marketing associate, they are risking the implementation of advertising and marketing strategy in the hands of somebody who's not an actual expert.

3. Hiring a marketing consultant will normally provide them with a multi-disciplinary team. Even a small service such as creating a social media page provides a vast choice of experience available at a moment's notice.

4. When a dental clinic hires a marketing consultant, they have an assurance that they are employing a team with total marketing expertise. This means that they do not need to reinvent the wheel and waste money on 'test and learn' tactics. A professional marketing consultant knows what works and does not work because they are backed by solid experience.

Your Job As A Marketing Consultant

As a marketing consultant your job is to help your client maximize their marketing returns, you are responsible for providing the best ROI for each client by helping them make as much sales as possible.

You as a marketing consultant will be responsible for creating, editing or monitoring the advertisements, you can also recommend the changes to fit the client's image as well as align to the marketing strategy of the client. You are responsible for formulating a sound sales and marketing strategy to maximize sales.

You will be handling a team for each client that will perform following functions:

An expert content writer who also can write effective sales copy, his job is to create eye catching content.
An expert designer to design custom graphics for marketing campaigns, he could also be hired on a freelance basis.
You will also require a web developer to design client's website, he will also be responsible to add functionality to the website, landing pages, and blogs.

To better understand your role as a marketing consultant, the work is broken into various modules. You will be spending your maximum time in the following areas.

Attending and organizing meetings with the client.
Complete Project management.
Overseeing the task of copywriting and editing of the content.
Monitoring the regular updating of web content.

Reporting to the client.

Attending and organizing meetings with the client.

Each week, as a marketing consultant, you will be required to meet with clients to:

Present your report on analytics; you will prepare a graph highlighting the sources of traffic, their origin, the sections of website receiving maximum traffic, how many posts are shared on social media etc. Update the client on the progress of ongoing projects. If some new development has been noticed by you, like a competitor launching a new promotional scheme, you will discuss the same with the client. Brainstorm any other ideas to maximize the returns on campaigns.

Complete Project management.

Project management is extremely vital component of your job. You will be responsible for assigning work to the team members, and updating the client about the progress on the project. You will have to oversee the creation of content, editing the same and getting it approved by the client. Your role is to ensure the smooth functioning of the team. You will be a liaison between the client and team members. Sometimes your job might take a role of administrator, but without you, the team will have no idea on how to proceed on the project. You will also be responsible for analyzing the results on a weekly basis and if you have to make adjustments, then you can suggest the same to the client.

Overseeing the task of copywriting and editing of the content.

You will be required to monitor the writer, who is responsible for creating content, in every client's marketing team. The job of the writer is to create the client's content as per the agreed specifications each month and you will review the same to make sure it's exactly as per the strategy approved by the client. This enables you to focus on generating maximum ROI in the client's marketing strategy and ensuring the success of campaign.

You will also be responsible for writing a pre-scheduled email to send to a list of leads that have filled up some form on a website. This will ensure that the leads are followed-up and turned into the sales cycle to complete the sales target.

Assessing Your Client

Marketing is a key to the success of business whether it is a fast food centre or a dental clinic. To help a dental clinic to grow, A dentist should have 200-300 visiting new patients each month. And to draw new dental patients, a clinic must provide a competitive product at competitive prices, together with convenient superior solutions -- all backed with a strong dental marketing program.

When attempting to work out the strategies on how to maximize advertisements for dental clinic, your must first perform the SWOT analysis. SWOT analysis stands for strengths, weaknesses, opportunities, and Threats. You must first list all the strengths and weaknesses and find out the competitive edge that you're able to maintain and leverage to make your practice stick out from the competitors. You have to be as brutally honest about your assessment so that you are able to recognize and cope with any barriers. Assess each item to ascertain what you may make the most of.

You can ask following questions to assess the strength and weakness about your client.
Which are the strongest areas in the business?
Define the process or service that gives you advantage over your competitors.
What kind of customer base the clinic has?
How does this clinic differentiate itself from other clinics?
How skilled is the staff in the areas of operation, customer service and handling pressure?
Do the employees of the company share the same vision?

In the same way you can explore the weaknesses of the clinic
What areas do you need improvement on?
What are the things that your competitors have edge over the clinic?
How does your clinic score in the marketing compared to the competitors?
Does your competitor have better visibility in the market?

As Soon as these questions are answered, you will be in a position to ascertain the dental marketing plan that will help your client to get ahead of the competition. .
Referrals are very strong medium increase the customers, but in a dental clinic very few customers see the clinic as a business, hence it becomes very tricky to ask the customer for referrals, yet you can design a customer satisfaction survey form and politely encourage the customer by asking if he would like to refer someone to the clinic. Usually established dental clinics get over 60% of business by referrals. You could surprise a client that has referred someone to the clinic by rewarding him with rebate or discount on his next visit. This kind of bonus has lot of intangible value and makes the client feel special. This small step goes a long way in building loyalty for the business. If you plan to offer rebates and discounts as a bonus then you can design a referral brochure that customer can fill up at his convenience, though care must be taken that a customer is not bothered for referrals. This works like providing incentives to the employees for contributing for the clinic in various ways.

Modern dental clinics have become market oriented due to easy availability of information on internet. If a person searches for a dental clinic near him, he will be flooded with the choices, and this forces the dental clinics to approach marketing with a professional attitude. Majority of marketing campaigns target women because they are major influencers when it comes to dental care products and clinics. A woman requires excellence in all aspects, not just products, but even service provided must be of world class. If your dental clinic campaign appeals to woman then you have better chance of acquiring new customers.

Prepare a Free Report

Offering a free marketing report to your customer is a great way of making them like you!

In terms of effort that you have to put in, it is little more than a summarizing your efforts in researching a client's website, and applying some of the ideas that we will discuss below. If your circumstances permit, you can offer them the free report and also spend time researching by asking them further questions whilst you put it together. The initial engagement with your client is discussed in the next chapter. The free report will be there to facilitate your initial engagement.

You will have to put in some time and not get paid. Creating the report will involve taking those issues that you identify with the restaurant, and matching them up with some solutions. You should be aiming for a tailor made document that is focused and gives great insight for the client. You will be suggesting ways to improve their business.

You must remember that the report needs to be easily understood by the client. Highlighting some of the defects in their marketing strategy and suggesting some improvements is all it needs to do. The report doesn't need to be comprehensive. It should just give the business owner a good idea of the things that need to be done in order to grow their business.

For your client, they are getting a valuable document for FREE! Lots of businesses pay consultants to do work like this for them, and you are offering it to them for nothing! You are going to make money by putting your solutions into practice for them. That is why you are giving them the results of your hard work.

You are showing the client that you want to help them and will add value. All businesses are averse to spending more. They will be open to listening to you when you have given them something valuable for free. You are acting in good faith and putting in effort before you get paid.

Now you won't have to do a 'hard sell' to your client. They will listen to you because you have started building a relationship. It feels so much better to call the client and say that you have done some research into their business and want to share it with them, rather than just trying to sell them something from the start.

Business owners usually aren't experts with marketing. When you show this report to them they should respond positively, often they will appreciate your advice. You can easily approach them using this tool; it will help you to build a positive relationship.

Planning for expansion

As a Freelancer, you have to plan for the Growth and Recruitment of employees ahead. If you're planning to recruit employees then you need to follow this section. Workers, both contractual and a permanent may be redeemed through online job sites, putting an ad in local papers. Additionally, you want to have a clearly defined role for a worker that aligns with your organization's vision.

If Your Company is expanding, It's a good indication, but you must carefully plan the recruiting process, this way you'll have ample time to pick the candidates that could end up being the assets of the organization. However, the hiring also expects that you, as an entrepreneur has to know about certain laws as you don't want any issues on the legal front. It may be that you may not call for the full-time employee, and decide to employ an independent contractor, no matter what you do, but the misclassification between an employee and an independent contractor may have grave consequences.

You must apply for EIN, this number is like asocial security number for your business. This is mandatory since it helps the income tax department to assess whether the tax liabilities are settled, whenever you have obtained EIN, you may create an application for employee withholding tax.

The other important thing to consider while hiring a worker is to be sure that you are hiring someone who's qualified to work your own country. Every new employee is needed to sign firm I-9 with all the necessary documents. When you complete the above formalities, you can issue a work offer letter that spells the job description together with terms of occupation. As your company grows, you'll also need a payroll provider to keep normal records.

As an entrepreneur you have to have the understanding of W-4 and W-2 forms.
You will need to keep the records of the tax withholding for at least three years, but you must remember that the W-4 Form needs to be filled by a worker before his tax status changes.

Approaching A Client

You have to rehearse your sales script about 5 times; the reason being a fantastic opener is necessary and you have to thoroughly memorize it. Despite not making a sale you will feel competent to talk about your experience and it can be tremendously beneficial in boosting your confidence.

You Have to try to come up with a decent opener, the best way to do This is by experimenting with what provides you the best answer. Memorize it and implement on a dummy prospect first without memorizing the script.

Even if you are an Introverted individual, competence gives you confidence clearly so don't beat yourself up on trying to act confident. Try to memorize the script, rehearse it in front of mirror, it is meant to boost your competency as a sales person, and consequently boosting your confidence in pitching your customers. While calling the customer for the first time you have to focus on controlling the dialogue.

You have to strive to find better leads.

You must accept rejections as a part of a business.

Another mistake that you may be making is that you are not being honest with your intentions; you must frankly tell the client the reasons for your calling him and what you are offering, and appeal to their logic why they ought to speak with you. It has to be remembered that a purchase is barely ever made by the client on the first contact when cold calling.

You'll be typically required to follow-up on telephone 5-7 times without sounding desperate. Your focus needs to be on triggering the desire which causes someone to purchase that product/service.

Until you reach the point where the client sees you as a solution provider that can fix a specific problem, you don't make a dime so that the entire approach ought to be focused on the on the client's needs or wants.

Do not appear like you've rehearsed the script. The best you can do is to just talk like a human. You shouldn't only aim for sale but also concentrate on building a relationship with your prospective customer.

Marketing Strategies you can recommend to your clients

The first step in convincing your client is to research the competition, though your client can give approximate assumptions on the practice of dentistry. You can ask them to allocate some amount to do blind shopping in other clinics. This will give you access to the various schemes launched by the competitors to attract new customers. You can help your client find out what are the things that his competitors are doing better. You must also hire someone to sign up at various websites to receive regular offers and ways to incorporate them in your client's marketing campaigns.

You can also ask your client to become actively involved in the community. You can help your client to organize free dental check-up camps in schools, or sponsor some local event. This kind of social interaction creates goodwill and positive reputation for your client's business.

If your client specializes in cosmetic dentistry or pediatric dentistry, then the advertising campaigns must target those specific groups of patients looking for cosmetic dentistry. If the campaign is haphazardly managed then it could end up targeting wrong group of customers and result in unnecessary expenses.

Make sure to use geo-targeting adverts on internet. This is the best way to target the people who have recently shifted into the locality. Most of the people who have recently relocated would turn to internet to search for something in their area because they might not have local friends yet, it is fast becoming a trend to check the ratings and reviews of the business on the internet before the customer decides to the try the services.

Many advertising agencies make the mistake of crafting ads that present too much information in too little space. This not only makes the advert look cluttered but it also leads to confusion in the mind of the customer. People do not have time to bother deconstructing the advertisements. As a marketing consultant you must ensure that the advertisements have a clear message and highlight only those services for which your client is spending money. For example, your client might not spend a fortune to advertise his dental cleaning service, he would spend money to advertise his specialty in cosmetic dentistry, so your campaign must have a clear message or offer about cosmetic dentistry.

You must also ensure the presence of your client's image and the images of his staff in website, a social media posting, postcards, brochures, etc. This creates a sense of comfort in the mind of customer.

Direct mail is Just Another marketing tool that many marketers think is dead. The statistics show that 60% individuals open direct mail as soon as they receive it. Direct email is ideal tool for creating brand awareness; create positioning of your product, sending rebates and offers to keep the customer. A direct mail campaign involves a higher conversion rate of approximately 3.5 percent when compared with meager 0.33 percent of email. Whenever you are interacting via direct mail, make sure it's a fun to read, you have to make best efforts to capture the eye of customer. Direct mail can be an ideal tool in contrast to email for generating the referrals because of greater response rate.

Radio advertising is a great way to capture the attention of a prospective client. A radio station has a staff to assist people in making decisions related to advertising. It's possible to talk to the sales staff of the radio Channels, and every radio stations have one or two less popular channels, so you are in a position to bargain hard for airtime. If your client decides to advertise on radio, always concentrate on the linear advertisements. If you don't understand, linear advertisements then these are the advertisements that are read by the radio personalities themselves. These are short ads and are really cheap compared to one minute advertisement. Linear advertisements give tremendous boost to the credibility to the advertising campaign.

Be active on social media. This interaction will probably cost you nothing; it's a kind of networking with people. Social networking has the capability to reach tens of thousands of people in a brief time, if you recognize how to use this platform. You will need to post often; this creates routine interaction with your prospective customers. You can even discuss the movies of your merchandise; be certain to be busy on social media. If somebody remarks then make certain to reply courteously. You may even have the chance to turn the negative comments to positive one by accepting or apologizing to the client. You may even create a competition for people to participate and win prizes. Social media can help you construct a new worth.

Magazines are still a powerful way to reach your potential Clients; you will find magazines who will write a editorial to your company if You put an advertisement together. Editorials are powerful piece of content and they may have an extremely positive impact on readers.

It is very difficult to convince people the importance of repetitiveness in a marketing campaign. Big corporations successfully utilize the power of repetition to attract customers. One of the cheapest and most effective ways of communicating with customers is to send them a postcard. Why postcard, you may wonder. People love to receive postcards, they prefer postcard over an email or any other form of digital communication.

Some people think of postcard as a bad marketing idea, but people love to sift through their mailboxes. You can send 5 emails, but chances are that this will make it look spammy, but if you send a postcard every two months, there are high chances of people converting into new customers. Another benefit of sending a regular postcard is that people will remember your client when they need a dentist. The key to success lies in consistency. This has an added benefit too, this will make people curious and they will search more about your client's business on Internet which could lead to increase in organic leads because people are likely to click on the name of your client because they are familiar with their name due to postcards.

Today marketing has become sophisticated. There are so many channels like social media, pay per click advertising, banners, billboards, flyers, etc. It becomes overwhelming task for a marketer to effectively utilize each channel. Even if he is able to utilize all options available to him, it would mean setting aside huge budget for marketing alone.

You could advice your client to opt for Geo-targeted advertisement on Internet Geo-targeted advertisements are best way to reach potential clients in the locality that your client operates. People repeatedly see the banners, advertisements of client's name cropping up. This kind of repetition makes people familiar and subconsciously they begin to give him preference over other clinics. The repetition will increase the reach of your client exponentially without making any extra effort or spending a fortune.

You must encourage your client to engage more with the customers. This way the bond between your client and his customers become stronger. This also builds an element of trust. Usually people tend to have some kind of fear visiting a dentist. You must encourage your client to put their clients to ease. You must ask your client to post his happy pictures with his clients, this kind of pictures serve as a social proof, and plays very important part in building trust element.

How To Generate Word of Mouth Buzz

The most important thing a business can do is to make people talk about your business -- your current clients. The clinic's clients are influential women and men who've maximum legitimacy. The toughest part is to convert happy and satisfied customers into new ambassadors.

Individuals which are generally pleased with the service are the ones that could spread a word. To leverage talkers, you need happy customers. As a marketing consultant your focus must be to design fascinating topics for customers so that they can chat about your client in their peer group.

Your job as a marketing consultant is to provide them the resources to get this done. You can convince your clients to create online courses; you can help your client to set-up Facebook page where they could chat about you. Your Facebook page can become an ideal platform to provide your client's customers tools and opportunities which help them spread the word about your business. You can even advice your client to hold monthly contests with small prizes like offering them a restaurant coupon or a movie ticket as an incentive. You can even set-up a contest to encourage them to come up with catchy slogans, share their experiences about your client's clinic, or even design posters. The clients will engage with everything mentioned above only if the contest is intriguing.

Once your client has started the discussion about your client's clinic, you must strive to become part of the conversation. You must encourage people to post comments, ask questions on email, phone, or fanpage. His way you can solve their doubts or queries instantly. These kind of small gestures go a long way in building customer satisfaction. It is very important to keep track of what people are saying about your client's business. As a marketing consultant it is your responsibility to maintain the image of your client.

Occasionally you must design an offer just for the particular customer; you can let the customer know that the offer is specifically designed for him to reward his association with the clinic. This will delight a customer and it is safe to assume that they will be discussing this offer with their friends. A personalized approach always makes the customer feel special. Another method is to ask customer about what they want, most of the time you can discover a marketing idea from their wants, and if this happens then your client's customers will definitely spread a good word about your client.

You must advise your client to do things differently, for example, if you can offer free coffee to them while they are waiting, they are surely going to discuss this because they view it as a special treatment. Marketing is all about differentiating one from others. You can also advise your clients to take pictures of happy customers along with a line or two as a testimonial and post it to your social media accounts. Such steps go a long way in generating a positive buzz about the business.

If done properly, it is not difficult to harness the power of word of mouth advertising. Remember word of mouth advertising is all about happy and satisfied customers.

Harnessing The Power Of Testimonials

You will be amazed to know that if you advice your clients to ask for a testimonial, you will realize that majority of customers will be completely thrilled to provide one because, remember, the dental clinic has helped them somehow.

I would like to remind you of just how many times you have completed a feedback form after purchasing a product in a shop or site. Leaving comments goes hand-in-hand along with purchase. The only thing is that virtually all opinions on shopping sites seem highly mechanical.

If you are want to ask a customer for his opinion, you can simply say that you merely demand a succinct sentence or short paragraph so the customer knows that this will not be taking plenty of his time.

To get the most from your testimonials, here are some of smart things you can do.

Only ask a Couple of customers at a time for a Testimonial.

Try to aim to ask a couple of customers each week or every 2 weeks. Usually when a customer says something about a product or business, it means that whatever people are saying --even if it's bad or good -- is normally authentic.

70 percent of people have faith on recommendations given by other individuals that they know and 40 percent have faith in recommendations from complete strangers! It strengthens the belief that people have a

penchant to trust independent testimonials, probably more than advertisements messages created by the business itself.

Apparently, the testimonial, however great, is useless unless your customers are saying great things! Besides being optimistic, marketable reviews, they also must to be brand new. The more recent the review, the larger the impact it could have, because prospective clients can see that you're still in business and offering a fantastic service even right now. You might have done something beautiful 3 decades ago, but it doesn't mean anything today...

Though written testimonials are important, they could be thought of fake. However, you can't deceive a person that is facing a camera. Video reviews are interactive and personal and score over written reviews by a huge margin. Videos make a memorable impact on people who are viewing them. 65 percent of the movie audience will see at least 3/4 of a film and 80 percent of those who have watched a movie online have the capacity to recall its content for a time of about 30 days later! Hence, you must try to get a video testimonial.

More Books In The Series

FROM BROKE TO BANK: STEP BY STEP GUIDE TO SURVIVE AS COPYWRITER

FROM BROKE TO BANK: STEP BY STEP GUIDE TO PET SITTING BUSINESS

FROM BROKE TO BANK: STEP BY STEP GUIDE TO DIGITAL MARKETING CONSULTING BUSINESS

www.ingramcontent.com/pod-product-compliance
Lightning Source LLC
Chambersburg PA
CBHW032311240526
45464CB00023BA/2985